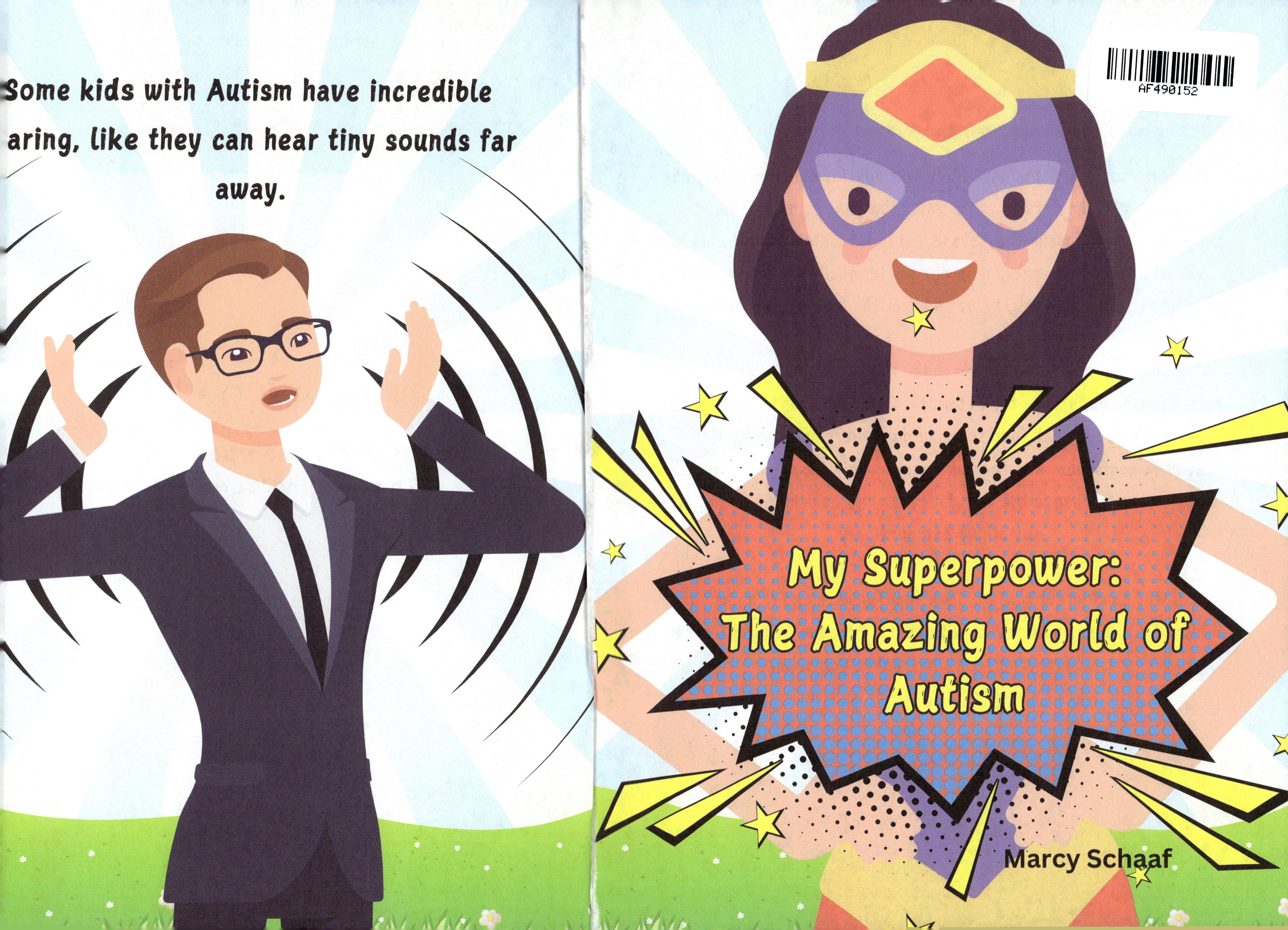

Some kids with Autism have incredible
aring, like they can hear tiny sounds far
away.
My Superpower:
The Amazing World of
Autism
Marcy Schaaf
AF490152

Every person is unique, with their own special abilities that make them who they are. But did you know that some kids have superpowers that make them stand out in incredible ways? Kids with Autism are like superheroes in our world, each with a special gift that helps them see, hear, and feel the world differently.

This book is about discovering those superpowers. Whether it's a talent for music, an eye for detail, or a heart full of kindness, these superpowers can lead to amazing careers and incredible achievements. Just like famous people who've used their Autism superpowers to change the world, every child has the potential to do something extraordinary.

So, let's celebrate these unique superpowers and imagine the incredible things you can do with yours. Because being different isn't just okay–it's what makes you super!

With this superpower, they could be amazing sound engineers or musicians, like Amadeus Mozart!

Others can remember everything they see or hear, like having a super vision!

This super memory can make them great historians or researchers, like Temple Grandin!

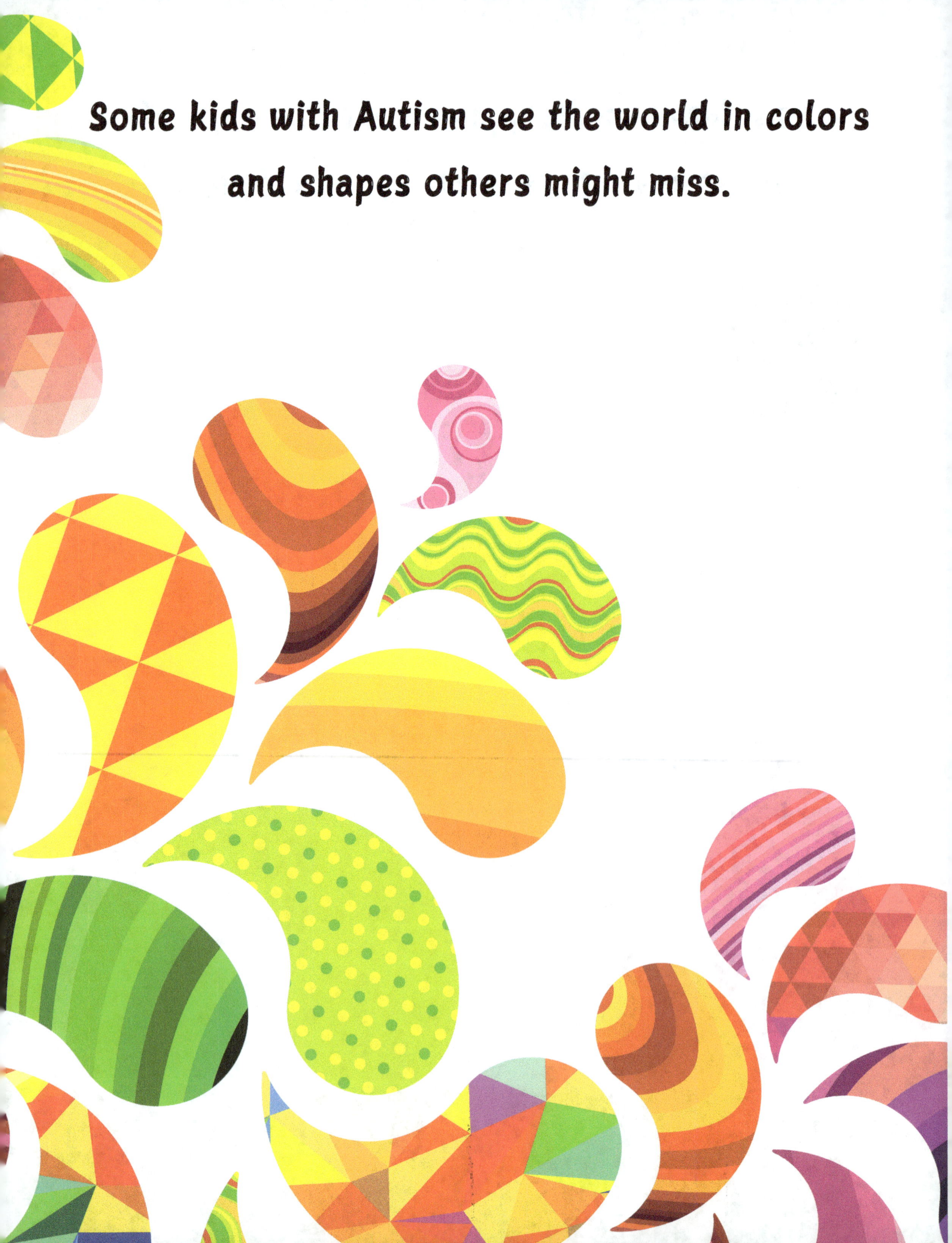

Some kids with Autism see the world in colors
and shapes others might miss.

They could become fantastic artists, designers, or architects, like Frank Lloyd Wright!

Some kids with Autism are amazing at solving puzzles, like superheroes with super smarts.

They might grow up to be engineers or
computer programmers, like Satoshi Tajiri,
creator of *Pokémon!*

Others might have a super sense of touch, feeling textures that others don't even notice.

This could make them skilled in fashion design, carpentry, or even as chefs, like Chef Christine Ha!

Some have a super love for animals, understanding them better than anyone else can.

They could become veterinarians or animal trainers, like Temple Grandin, who transformed the livestock industry!

Others might be super listeners, hearing every word and making you feel heard and loved.

This could lead them to careers in counseling or teaching, like Dr. Vernon L. Smith, an economics professor!

Some kids with Autism have an amazing talent
for music, like they were born to play!

They might become professional musicians,
like Glenn Gould, the famous pianist!

Others might have a super love for numbers,
solving math problems like a superhero.

They could grow up to be mathematicians or financial planners, like Daniel Tammet, a savant with incredible math skills!

Some kids with Autism can notice every little detail, like real-life detectives.

This skill could make them great detectives, editors, or quality control inspectors, like Saga Noren from the TV Series "The Bridge"

Others have a superpower of kindness, always caring and helping those around them.

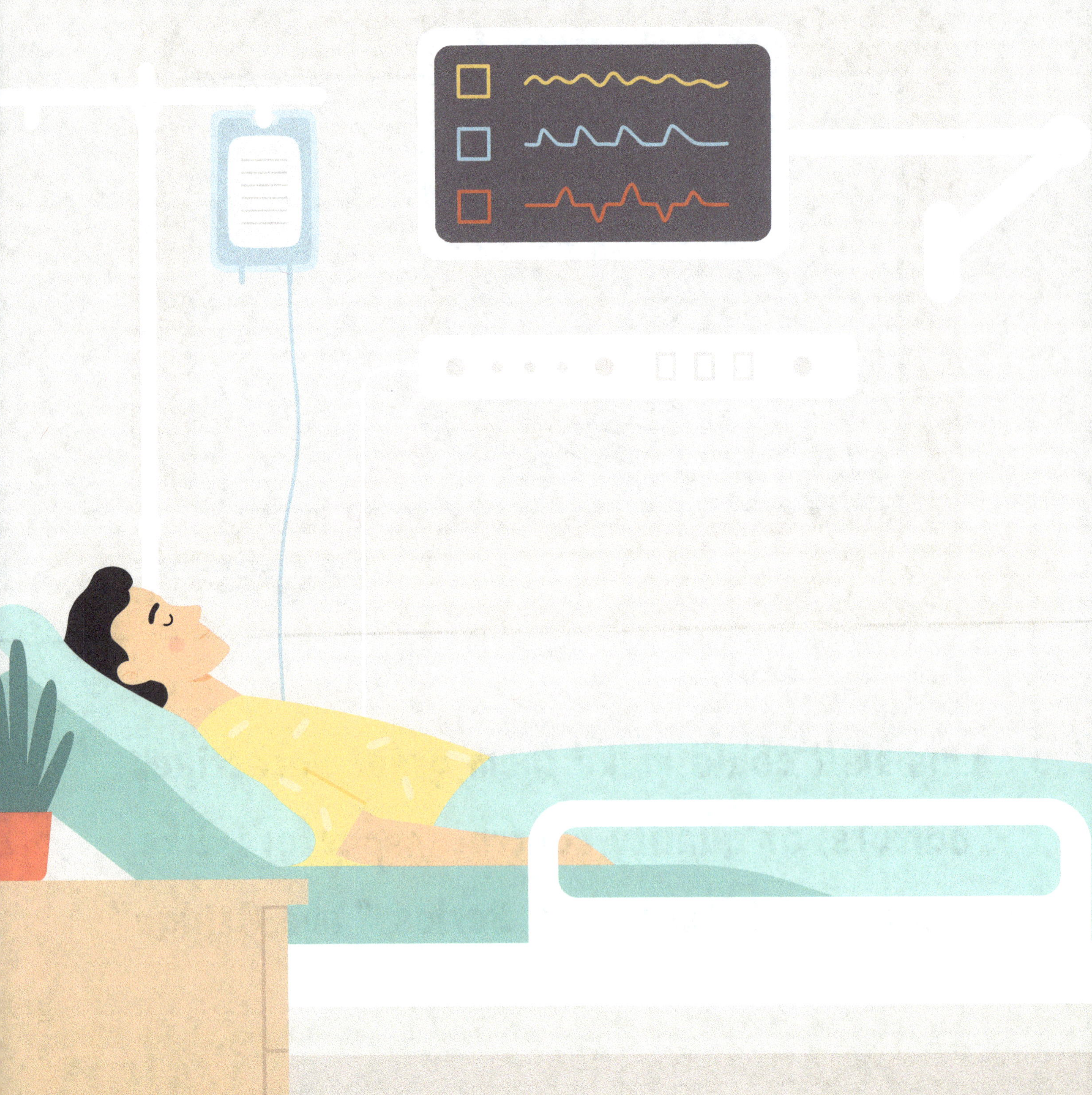

They could become nurses, social workers, or community organizers, like Amy Gravino who's advocacy has inspired many in the medical field.

Some kids with Autism are super storytellers,
imagining worlds full of adventure and fun.

They could grow up to be authors or filmmakers, like Tim Burton, the visionary director!

Every child with Autism has their own unique superpower, leading to exciting careers.

Their superpowers make the world a brighter, more colorful, and interesting place.

No matter what your superpower is, it's important, and it can lead to an awesome career!

Everyone is different and that's what makes each of us a superhero in our own way.

So, find your superpower, dream big, and
imagine all the amazing things you can do!

The End

Books By Schaaf

www.BookBySchaaf.com

Find us at: